SUPER BOWL

ST. LOUIS RAMS

CHAMPIONS

SUPER BOWL

Published by Creative Education

123 South Broad Street

Mankato, Minnesota 56001

Creative Education is an imprint of The Creative Company.

DESIGN AND PRODUCTION BY **EVANSDAY DESIGN**

LIBRARY OF CONGRESS CATALOGING-IN-PUBLICATION DATA

LeBoutillier, Nate.

St. Louis Rams / by Nate LeBoutillier.

p. cm. — (Super Bowl champions)

Includes index.

ISBN 1-58341-390-1

1. St. Louis Rams (Football team)—Juvenile literature. I. Title. II. Series.

GV956.S28L43 2005

796.332'64'0977866—dc22   2005048363

First edition

9 8 7 6 5 4 3 2 1

COVER PHOTO: running back Marshall Faulk

PHOTOGRAPHS BY

Corbis (Bettmann), Getty Images (Elsa, Streeter Lecka, Jon SooHoo/Allsport, Rick Stewart /Allsport), Icon Sports Media Inc., SportsChrome USA

CHAMPIONS

ST. LOUIS RAMS

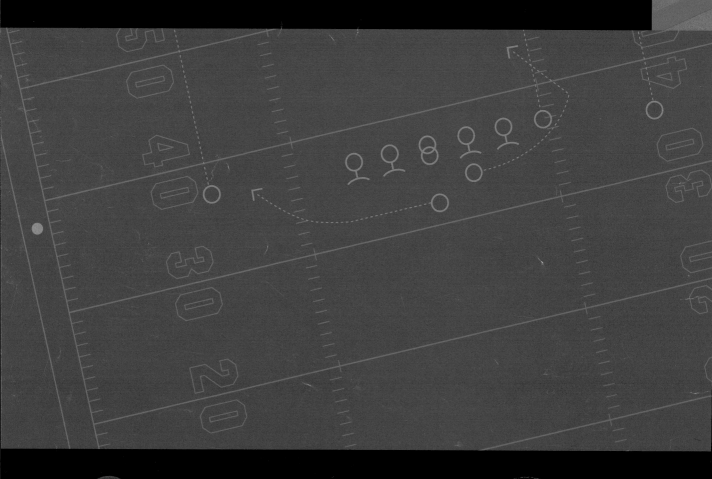

THE RAMS are a professional football team in the National Football League (NFL). They play in St. Louis, Missouri. St. Louis is sometimes called "The Gateway City." It is in the middle of the United States.

THE RAMS play in an indoor stadium called the Edward Jones Dome. Their helmets are blue with gold swirls on the side. The swirls look like horns. Their uniforms are gold, blue, and white. The Rams play many games against teams called the 49ers, Cardinals, and Seahawks.

THE RAMS played in Cleveland, Ohio, from 1937 to 1945. They were NFL champions their last year in Cleveland. Their best player was quarterback Bob Waterfield. Fans called him "The Rifle" because he was so good at passing the ball.

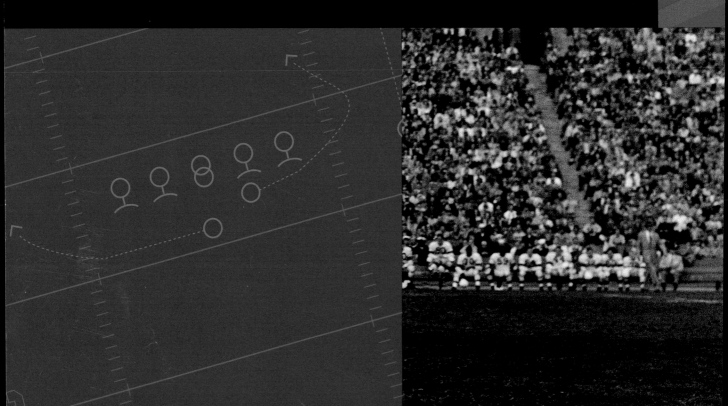

IN **1946**, the Rams moved to Los Angeles, California. They beat the Cleveland Browns in 1951 to win another world championship.

The Los Angeles Rams threw a lot of long passes in 1951 ^

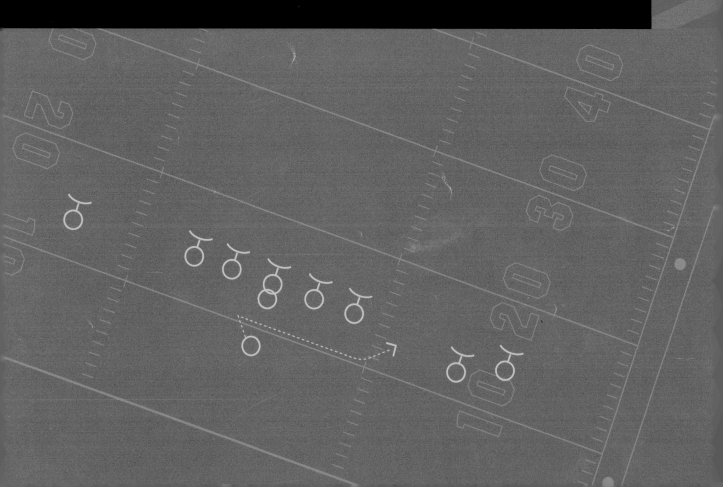

ERIC DICKERSON joined the Rams in 1983. He was a fast running back who made running for touchdowns look easy. In his first season, he ran for 2,105 yards. That is still an NFL record.

THE RAMS moved to St. Louis in 1995. They won their first game there. Fans in St. Louis were excited to have a new team in their city.

KURT WARNER was a good quarterback in college. But no NFL team wanted him. So he worked at a grocery store. But then the Rams signed him in 1999. He was voted the best player in the NFL that year.

I**N 1999**, the Rams got to the Super Bowl. Kurt Warner and fast running back Marshall Faulk helped the Rams beat the Tennessee Titans. That made them the world champions for the first time in 48 years!

ONE OF the Rams' best players today is Torry Holt. He is a very fast wide receiver. Rams fans hope that he will help lead the team back to the Super Bowl!

GLOSSARY

National Football League (NFL)

a group of football teams that play against each other; there are 32 teams in the NFL today

professional

a person or team that gets paid to play or work

record

something that is the best (or most) ever

signed

hired to play for a team

FUN FACTS

Team colors
Gold, blue, and white

Home stadium
Edward Jones Dome (66,000 seats)

Conference/Division
National Football Conference (NFC), West Division

First season
1937

Super Bowl win
1999 (beat Tennessee Titans 23–16)

Training camp location
Macomb, Illinois

NFL Web site for kids
http://www.playfootball.com